BK 168499 0

INVESTIGATING VOLUME

Ed Catherall

Wayland

Investigations

Investigating Areas
Investigating Graphs
Investigating Numbers
Investigating Sets
Investigating Angles
Investigating Shapes
Investigating Volume
Investigating Weight

First published in 1983 by Wayland Publishers Limited
49 Lansdowne Place, Hove, East Sussex BN3 1HF, England
© Copyright 1983 Wayland Publishers Limited
ISBN 0 85078 253 8

Illustrated and designed by David Anstey
Typeset by Tunbridge Wells Typesetting Services Ltd.
Printed in Italy by G. Canale & C.S.p.A., Turin
Bound in the UK by the Pitman Press, Bath

Contents

Chapter 1 Capacity

Making clay shapes 4
How much is a handful? 5
How many are in the jar? 6
Which bottle has the greatest capacity? 7
At the supermarket 8
Making a bottle collection 9
Cups and glasses 10
Measuring capacity 11
Measuring the flow of water 12
How much water is in your bath? 13
Investigating cars 14
Measuring liquids 15

Chapter 2 Volume

Making clay cubes 16
Making boxes 17
Making a tray 18
The volume of trays 19
Boxes at the supermarket 20
The volume of prisms 21
The volume of a page in a book 22
How much wood is in a tree? 23
Wrapping a present 24
The surface and volume of trays 25
The relationship of surface to volume 26
Metric volume and capacity 27

Chapter 3 Density

Measuring the volume of your hand 28
Measuring your lung capacity 29
Measuring the volume of a stone 30
Measuring density 31
The density of liquids 32

Chapter 1 Capacity

Making clay shapes

Roll a lump of modelling clay into a solid ball.
Use all of this ball of clay to form a solid clay cube.
Does the cube look the same size as the ball?
You used the same amount of clay to make the solid ball and the solid cube. The mass, or quantity, of clay is the same.

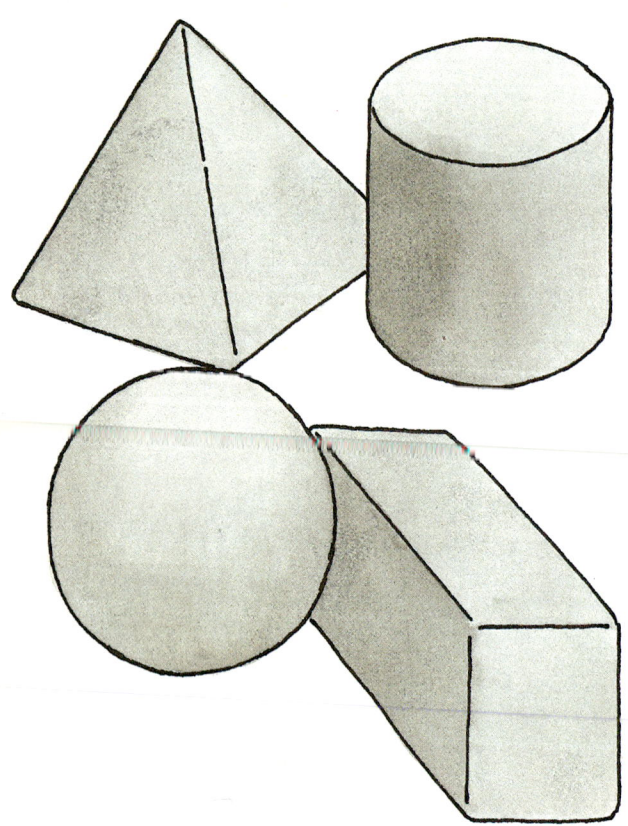

Roll your clay cube into a solid cylinder. Notice that although the shape changes, the quantity of clay is the same.
The total space that each clay shape takes up is its VOLUME.
The solid ball, the solid cube and the solid cylinder all have the same volume.

Make other solid shapes from your clay. Remember to use all the clay.
Every shape you make has the same volume.
Does any shape look larger than the other shapes?

How much is a handful?

Put many marbles into a bag.
If you do not have any marbles use beans, nuts or dried peas.

Grab a handful of marbles from the bag and carefully drop them into a bowl.
How many marbles can you grab?

Length

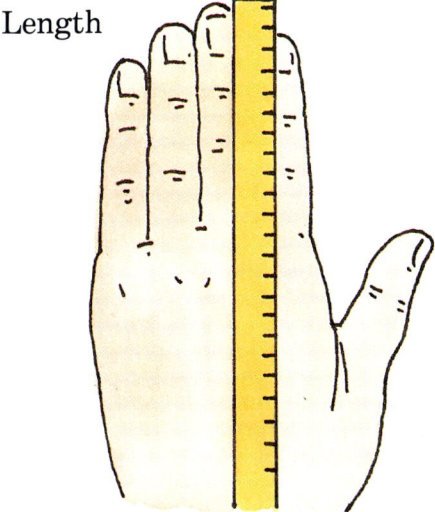

Grab another handful of marbles.
Can you grab the same number of marbles this time?
What is the largest number of marbles your hand will hold?
Can you grab more marbles with your right hand or your left hand?

Measure the length of your hand from your wrist to the tip of your largest finger.
Measure the span of your hand.
Are both your hands the same size?

Measure the length and the span of your friends' hands.
Does the friend with the largest hand grab the most marbles?

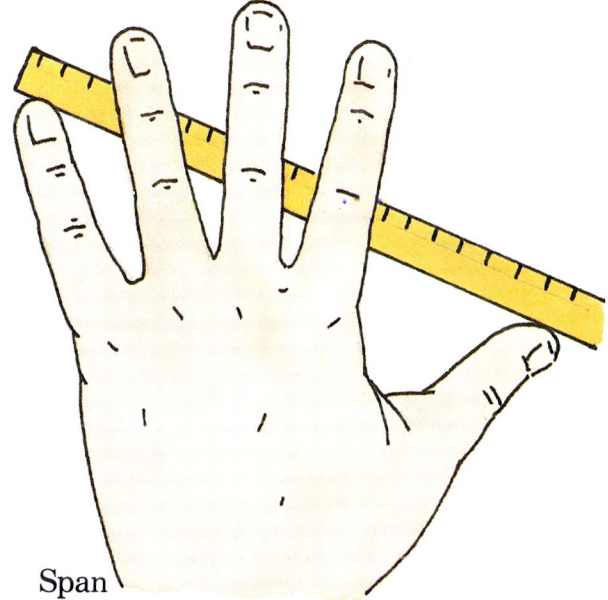

Span

How many are in the jar?

Put marbles in a glass jar until the jar is full.
How many marbles are there in the jar?
Can you get more marbles in the jar if you stack them carefully?

Ask your friends how many marbles they think there are in a full jar.
Notice how they try to arrive at an accurate guess.
What is the range of guesses?
Do your friends tend to overestimate or underestimate the number of marbles?
How close is the nearest guess?

Fill the same jar with dried peas.
How many peas are there in the jar?
Is it more difficult to estimate the number of peas in the jar?
Why is this?

Which bottle has the greatest capacity?

The capacity of a bottle is the amount it will hold. This is the same as the volume that it will hold.

Find many different bottles of similar (but not the same) capacity. Carefully inspect each bottle and arrange them in the order of their capacity.

Fill the bottle with the smallest capacity with water.
Place the bottle with the next smallest capacity in the sink.
Carefully pour the contents of the smaller bottle into the larger bottle.
Try not to spill any water.
How much more water is needed to fill the larger bottle?

Pour water from this larger bottle into the next bottle in order.
How much more water is needed to fill this third bottle?

Continue pouring the contents of each bottle into the next larger one.
Did you accurately arrange the bottles in order of their capacity?

At the supermarket

Are only liquids sold by capacity? What units of capacity can you find on the cartons and the bottles in your local shop?
List all the products that are sold by capacity rather than weight.

Which products do you think are most attractively packaged?
Are these luxury products?
Look along a row of shelves. Which product is most easily seen?
Why is this? On which shelf is the product displayed?

Look at bottles of cooking oil. What is the capacity of these bottles? Do bottles of the same capacity, but of different brands, look the same size? Are there any jars that appear to have a greater capacity than they actually have? Look at different brands of jam. What do you notice?

Notice the packaging of cosmetics.
In what ways do manufacturers make a small volume look larger?

Making a bottle collection

Start a bottle collection. Make sure that each bottle in your collection is empty and clean.
Do not keep cracked or broken bottles.

Find out all you can about each bottle. Record this information on a card. Display the card with the bottle.

Notice that bottles are made from different materials.
Glass bottles are made from different coloured glass.
Some bottles are transparent. Others are opaque.
How is each bottle capped?
Use a measuring cylinder or measuring jug to check the capacity of each bottle.

Notice that wine bottles have different shapes, and the shape often tells you the origin of its contents.
Milk bottles often have details of the dairy embossed in the glass.

Cups and glasses

How many glasses of different capacities can you find in your house?
Do any of these glasses have special names?
Do any of these glasses measure a particular amount of liquid?
Is this glass accurate?
How many teaspoonfuls of water does each glass hold?

Fill a bottle with water.
What is the capacity of the bottle?
How many times can you fill one glass from the bottle?
Test all the different glasses.
What do you notice?

How many cups of different capacities can you find in your house?
How many teaspoonfuls of water does each cup hold?

Measuring capacity

Find a straight-sided glass or plastic tumbler.
Cut a strip of paper the height of your glass.
Use sticky tape to fasten your paper strip vertically to the outside of the glass.

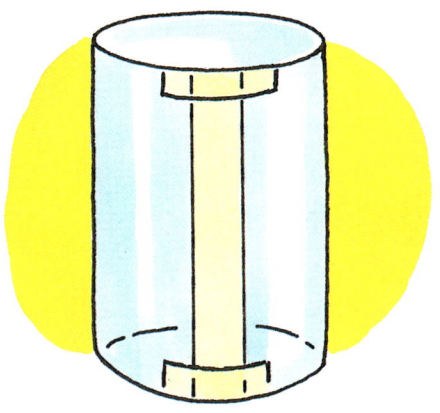

Stand the glass on a flat surface.
Put one tablespoonful of water into the glass.
Mark the water level on the paper strip.
Mark the water level each time you put a tablespoonful of water in the glass.
How many tablespoonfuls of water do you need to fill the glass?

Use your measuring glass to find the capacity of smaller glasses of water.

Do you have a measuring jug at home? What measuring scale is on the side of this jug?

Find or borrow a plastic measuring cylinder. Use this cylinder to work out a measuring scale for another glass or tumbler.

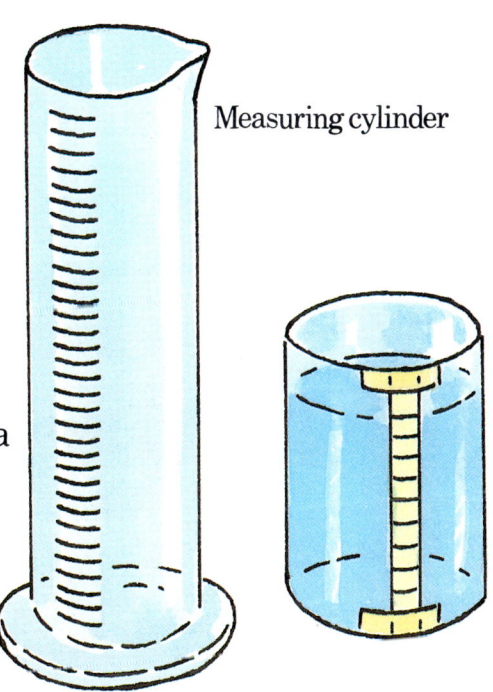

Measuring cylinder

Measuring the flow of water

Find a measuring cylinder or a measuring jug (see page 11).
Go to the sink and turn on the water until you have a small steady trickle of water.

Place your measuring cylinder under the stream of water for EXACTLY 10 seconds. How much water is in your measuring cylinder?
How much water is flowing into the cylinder every second?

Replace your measuring cylinder under the stream of water for another 10 seconds.
Does the same volume of water flow into your cylinder?
What is the rate of water flow every second?
Calculate how much water will flow in 30 seconds and in 1 minute.
Use your measuring cylinder to check to see if you are right.

Increase the water flow and repeat this exercise.

How much water is in your bath?

When you take a bath, how deep do you like the water?
Mark this level on the side of the bath.
Use buckets or a measuring jug to fill the bath to this level.
How much water do you have in your bath?

How much water do you put in the hand basin when you wash?

If you have a shower measure the amount of water that flows from the shower in 1 minute (see page 12).
How much water do you use when you take a shower?

Keep a record of the amount of water that you use in a week just for washing.
Try to estimate how much water your household will use in a week.
Where does this water come from?
Do you practise water conservation in your area?

Investigating cars

The next time you are in a car find out its make and model.
What is the size of the engine?
Find out how much fuel the car holds in its tank.
Ask how far this car will travel on 1 gallon or 1 litre of fuel.
This is the fuel efficiency of the car. The more fuel efficient a car is, the further it will go on a gallon or a litre of fuel.
Calculate how far the car will travel with a full tank.

Which cars are the most fuel efficient?
What is their engine size?
Which cars are the least fuel efficient?
What is their engine size?
What do you notice about engine size and fuel efficiency?

What can a driver do to improve the fuel efficiency of his car?

Making a tray

Use a ruler to draw a square with each side 8 cm long on a sheet of strong paper.
Use your ruler to divide each side into eight equal parts.
Join the marks together to form squares. (Picture 1)
How many 1 cm squares are there inside the large square?

Cut out the squares from each corner. (Picture 2)
Fold up the outer row of squares to form a tray. (Picture 3)

How many 1 cm cubes will your tray hold?
Cubes may not be piled on each other.
What is the volume of your tray?

Repeat this exercise. This time draw a square with sides 10 cm long.
Cut out the corner squares.
How many 1 cm cubes will this tray hold?
What is the volume of this tray?

What is the volume of a tray that you make from a square with sides 12 cm long?

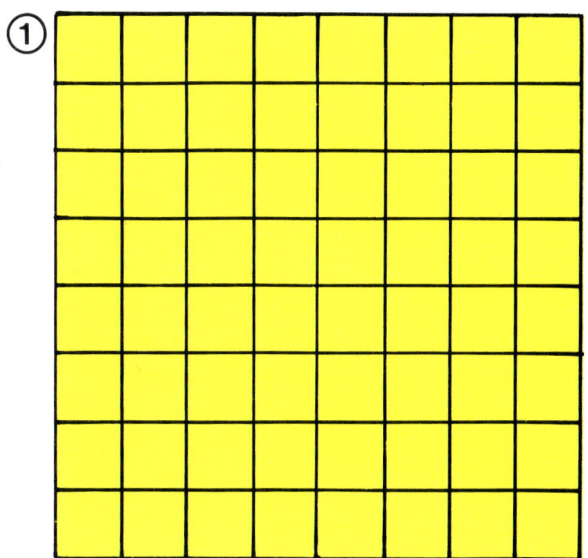

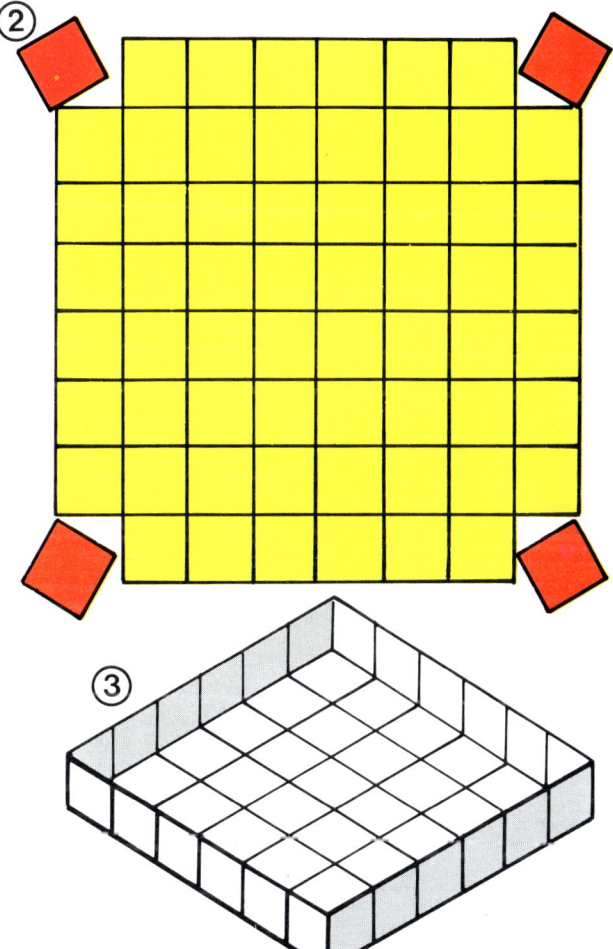

Making boxes

Draw five equal-sized squares on paper. (Picture 1)
Mark the square that will form the base of the box.
Cut out the shape containing the squares.
Carefully fold the paper along the sides of the squares to make an open box. (Picture 2)
After you have made the box, open the paper again and keep this shape.

Draw another shape containing five equal sized squares. (Picture 3)
Cut out this shape and fold it into a box.
Keep this shape.

Draw another shape containing five equal sized squares that will make a box.
There are eight different shapes containing five squares that will form a box.
Can you find the other six shapes?
Make sure you find different shapes, not shapes that are turned.
(Picture 4)

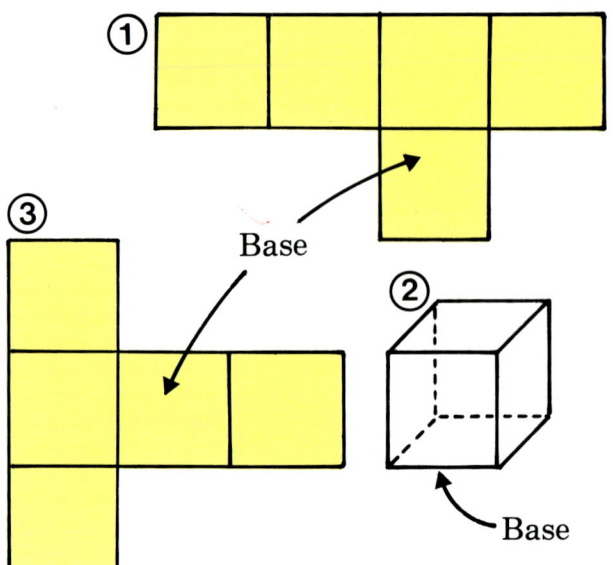

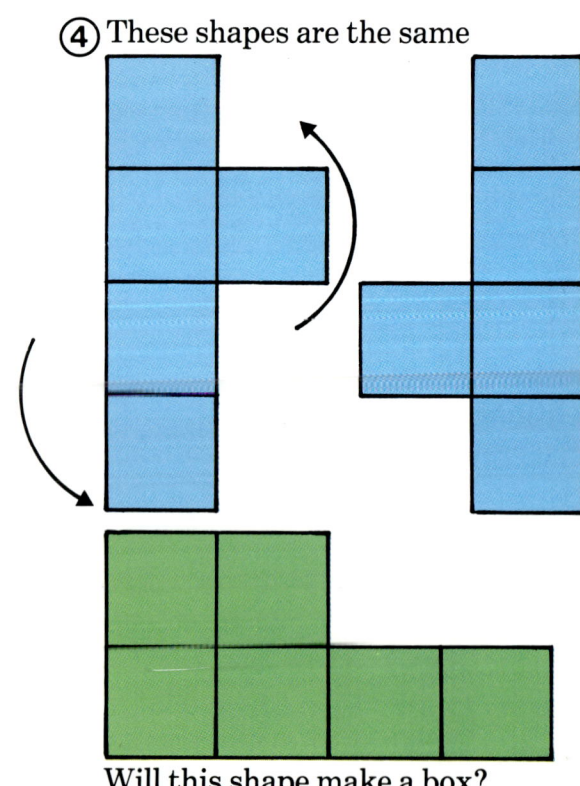

Will this shape make a box?

17

Chapter 2 Volume

Making clay cubes

Find a lump of modelling clay.
Use a ruler to carefully make a solid cube of clay with sides measuring exactly 1 cm.
Use a knife to carefully cut the sides for greater accuracy.
Notice that your 1 cm cube uses 1 cubic cm of clay.
The volume of your cube is 1 cubic cm.

Carefully make seven more 1 cm cubes of clay.
Compare the cubes to see that they are all the same size.
You have made eight 1 cm cubes.
The total volume of all the cubes is 8 cubic cm.

Arrange the cubes to form two rows of four cubes.
What is the length, width and height of this shape?

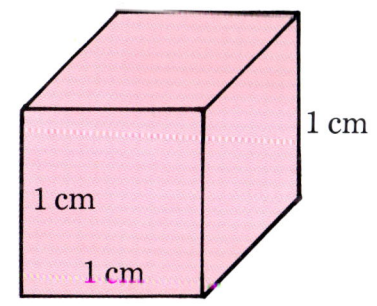

Arrange your eight cubes to form one larger cube.
What is the length, width and height of this larger cube?
What is the volume of this larger cube?

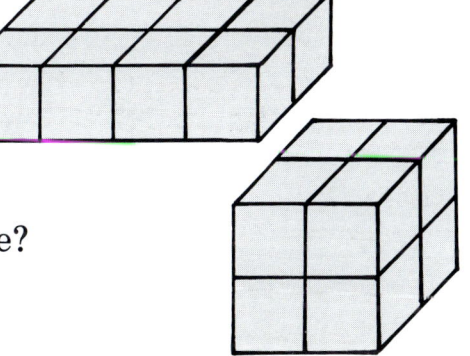

Roll all of your cubes together to make any shape. What is the volume of this shape?
Has altering the shape of the clay changed its volume?

Measuring liquids

Liquids are usually measured in litres, Imperial gallons or U.S. gallons.
Ten litres are equal to 2.2 Imperial gallons.
Ten litres are also equal to 2.6 U.S. gallons.
Which is larger, an Imperial gallon or a U.S. gallon?

Calculate what 20, 30, 40 and 50 litres would equal in Imperial gallons and in U.S. gallons.

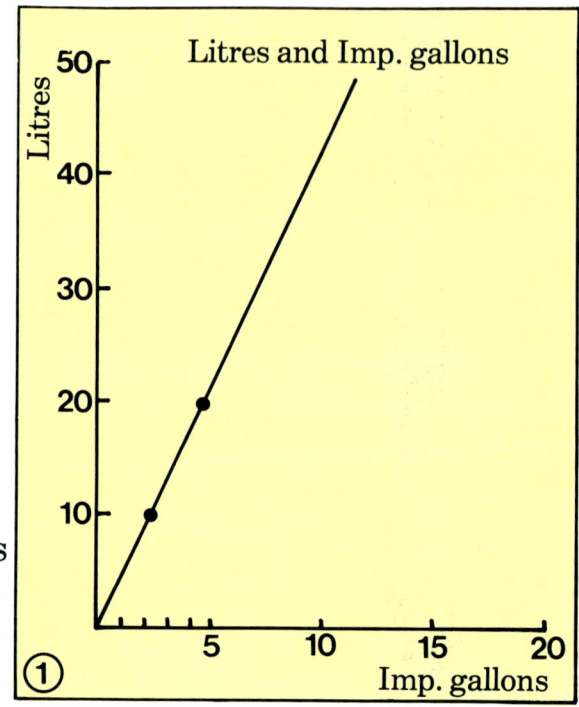

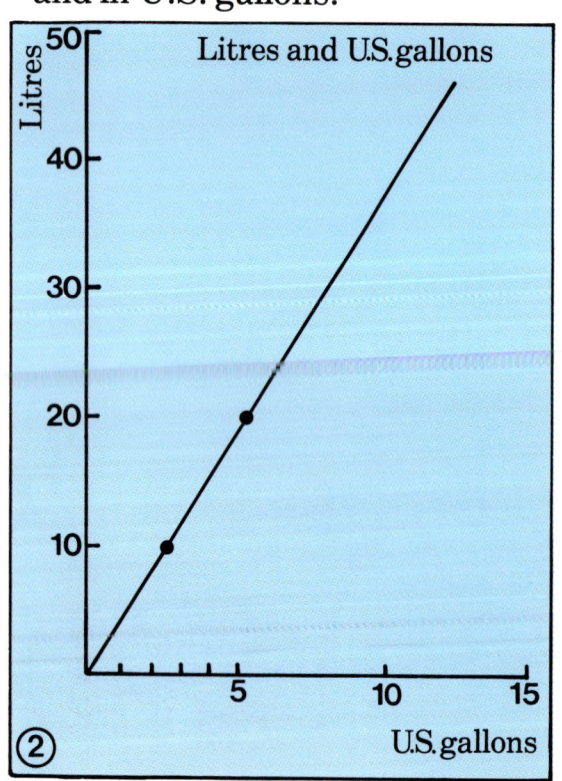

Use these figures to draw a conversion graph of litres and Imperial gallons. (Picture 1)
Use your graph to calculate how many litres are equal to 1, 5, and 10 Imperial gallons.

Draw a conversion graph of litres and U.S. gallons. (Picture 2)
Use your graph to calculate how many litres are equal to 1, 5, and 10 U.S. gallons.

15

The volume of trays

Make a square tray that will hold one layer of thirty-six 1 cm cubes (see page 18). What is the volume of this tray?

Notice that the base of the tray is a square 6 cm by 6 cm which is 36 square cm.

The height of the sides of the tray is 1 cm. You can calculate the volume by multiplying the area of the base by the height. Try it.

If you put another layer of thirty-six 1 cm cubes on top of the first layer, how many cubes are there in the tray?
What is the height of the sides of a tray that will hold two layers of cubes?
What is the volume of this new tray with higher sides?

If you put a third layer of thirty-six 1 cm cubes on top of the first two layers, how many cubes are there in the tray?
What is the height of the sides of this tray that holds three layers of cubes?
What is the volume of this tray with higher sides?

Boxes at the supermarket

Cuboids

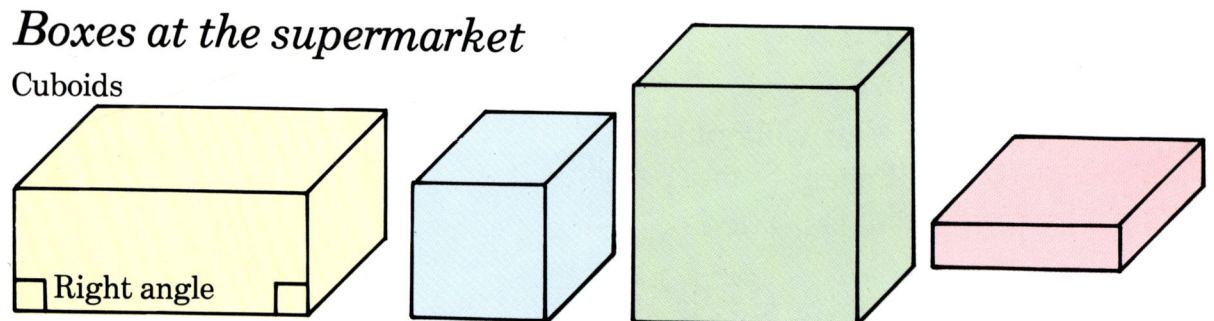

Find an empty box. Check that all the corners of the box are right angles. This box is a cuboid.

Use a ruler to measure the length and width of the base of the box.
Calculate the area of the base.
Measure the height of the box.
Calculate the volume of the box (see page 19).

Turn the box on its side. Notice the box looks different but the volume is the same. How can you prove this?

Find other boxes. Check that they are cuboids.
Measure the base of each box.
Measure the height of each box.
Calculate the volume of each box.
Do any of your boxes have different shapes but the same volume?

Calculate the volume of different boxes of cereal. What do you notice about the area of the base compared with the height of the box?
Are the boxes attractive if placed on their sides?

The volume of prisms

Use modelling clay to make a large solid clay cuboid (see page 20).
Use a ruler to calculate the volume of clay in your cuboid.
Record this volume.

A prism is a shape with its top and bottom surfaces the same size and shape, and its sides parallel.

Use your cuboid of clay to make a prism. Remember to use all of the clay.
Check that the sides are vertical.
Measure the height of one vertical side.
Measure the area of the base of your prism.
Notice that the volume of the clay stays the same.

When you cannot easily calculate the area of the base, then divide the volume of the clay by the height of this prism.
Remember that the area of the base multiplied by the height equals the volume. So the volume divided by the height will give you the area of the base.

Calculate the area of the base of different prisms.

Prisms

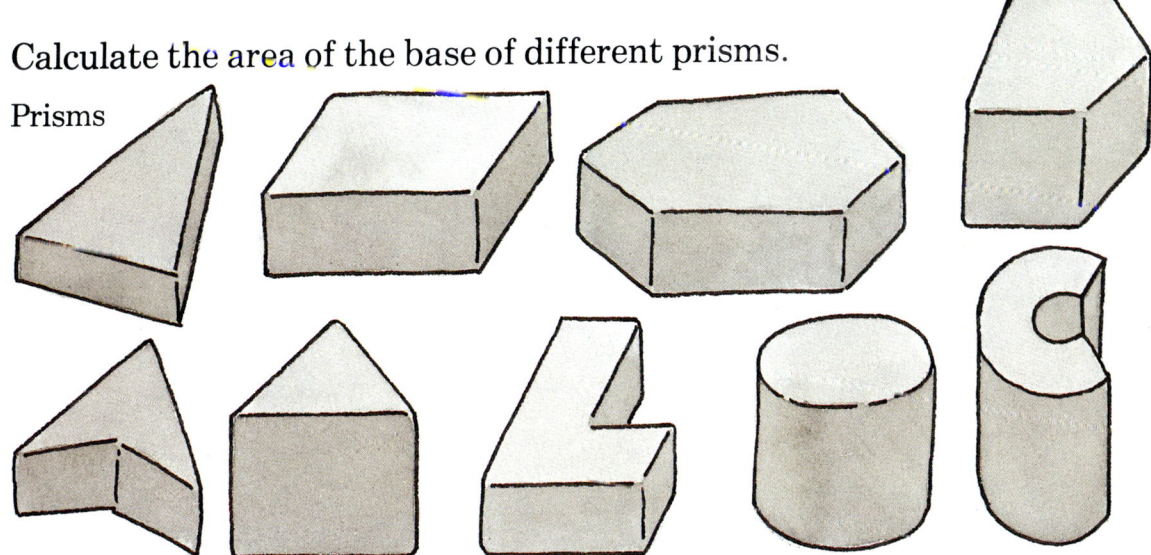

The volume of a page in a book

It is difficult to measure the volume of thin objects.
Find a thick book.
Measure the length and width of one page in the book.
What is the surface area of this page?
Try to measure the thickness of this page.
Try to calculate the volume of this page.

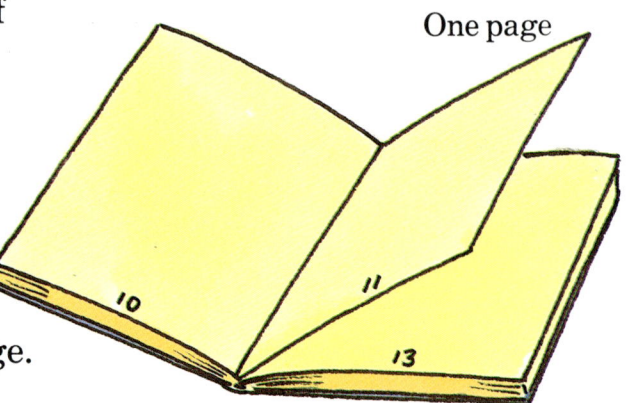
One page

Count twenty pages in the book.
Remember, each whole page will have two page numbers.
Tightly press together your twenty pages.
Measure the thickness of all twenty pages.
What is the volume of all twenty pages?
If you divide this volume by twenty, you can calculate the volume of one page.

Do the pages of different books have different thicknesses?

How much wood is in a tree?

Ask a friend to help you to measure a tree trunk.
Hold a ruler vertically at arm's length.
Be sure to keep your ruler and arm still.
Move back from your tree until the trunk appears to be as long as the ruler.
The trunk ends where the branches begin.
Stop and turn your ruler horizontally so that the ruler starts at the bottom of the trunk.

Ask your friend to pace out from your tree and stop her when she appears to be a ruler's length away from the tree.

How many paces did your friend take?
How many paces is the length of the trunk?
Measure the length of one of her paces.
How high is the tree trunk?

Measure the diameter of the trunk of your tree.
Halve this diameter to find the radius.
Multiply this radius by itself.
Multiply this answer by 3.14.
This is the area of one circle in your tree trunk.
Area = 3.14 × radius × radius
Multiply the area by the height to get the volume of your tree trunk.

D = Diameter

Wrapping a present

Find a cuboid box to hold your present.
What is the volume of your box?

How many sides or faces does your cuboid box have?
Measure the length and width of each face. What do you notice?
Calculate the area of each face.
What is the total surface area of your box? This is the sum of all the areas of all the faces.
How much area must your wrapping paper have in order to cover your box?
Remember to include enough area to fold your paper. The folding is usually done on the two smaller faces.

Find a larger cuboid box.
What is the volume of this box?
Measure the area of each face.
What is the total surface area of this larger box?
How much have you increased the volume by using this larger box?
How much have you increased the surface area by using the larger box?

The surface and volume of trays

Use a ruler to draw a square with each side 12 cm long on a sheet of strong paper (see page 18).
Use your ruler to divide each side into 12 equal parts.
Join these marks together to form squares. (Picture 1)
How many 1 cm squares are there inside the large square?

Cut out the square on each corner. (Picture 2)
Fold up the outer row of squares to form a tray. (Picture 3)
How many 1 cm cubes will your tray hold (see page 18)?
What is the volume of the tray?

Open your tray. Cut out a larger square from each corner. (Picture 4)
Fold up your paper to make a tray.
How deep are the sides of your tray?
How many 1 cm cubes will this tray hold?
What is the volume of this tray?

Continue to cut out larger squares from each corner.
Calculate the volume of each tray.
Which tray has the greatest volume?

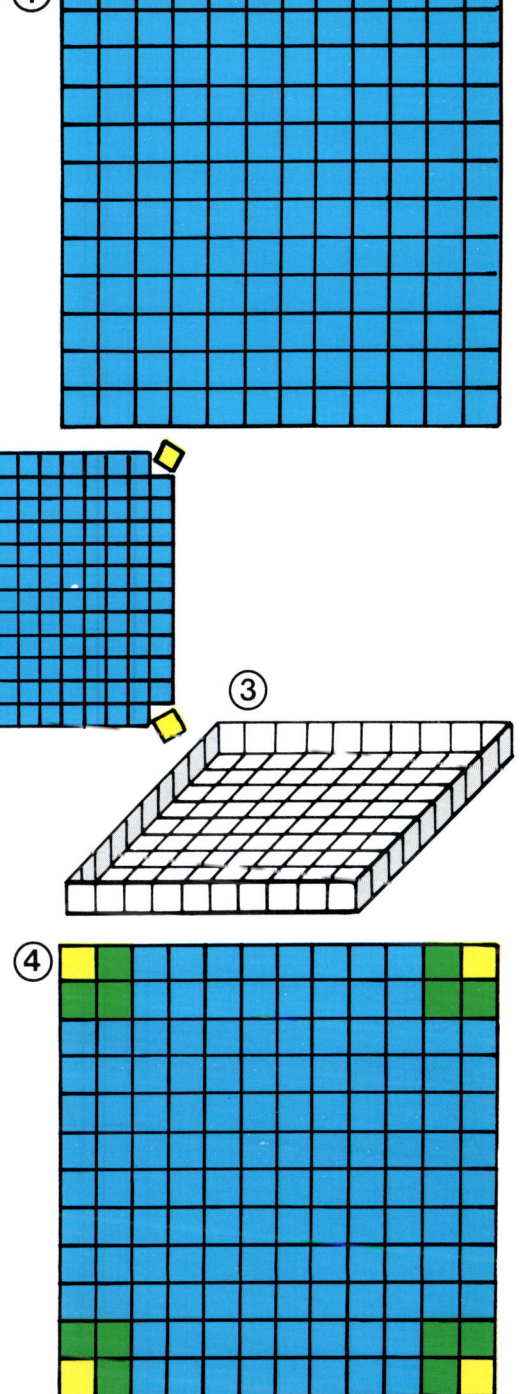

The relationship of surface to volume

Draw a picture of a 1 cm cube on a sheet of paper.
What is the volume of the cube?
How many sides or faces does the cube have?
What is the surface area of each face?
What is the total surface area of your 1 cm cube?

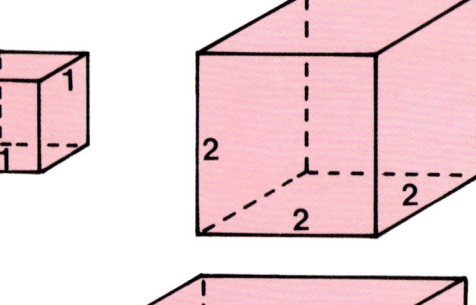

Draw a cube with each side 2 cm long.
What is the volume of this cube?
What is the surface area of one face?
What is the total surface area of this cube?

Draw a cube with each side 3 cm long.

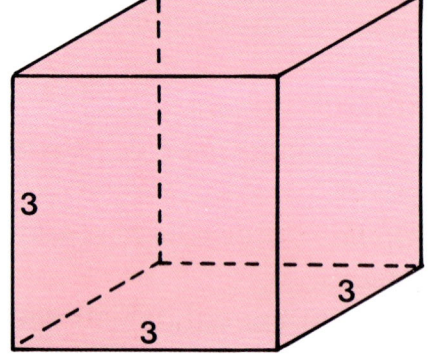

What is the volume of this cube?
What is the total surface area of this cube?

Find the volume and total surface area of cubes with sides 4 cm, 5 cm, 6 cm, and 8 cm long.
Notice how the volume and the surface area increase.
What do you notice?
Draw a graph showing the surface area and the volume of cubes.

Calculate the volume and the surface area of other cuboids.
Is the pattern similar?

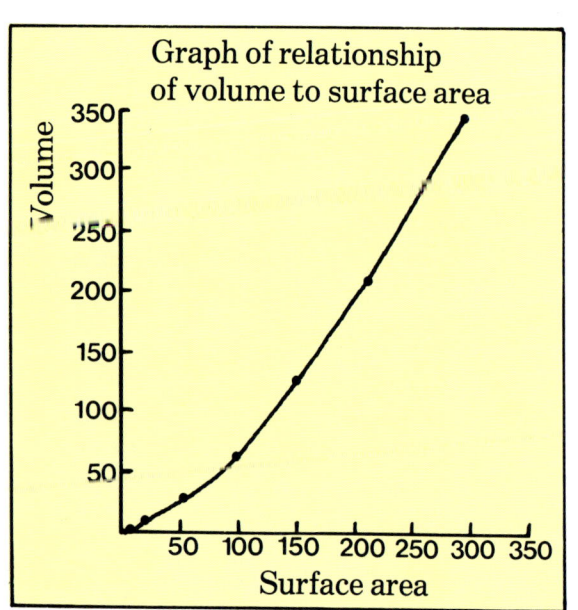

Metric volume and capacity

Measure the volume of your room.
What units of measurement do you use?
Measure the volume of your bath.
If you filled the bath to the brim how much water would it hold?

Measure the volume of a cereal box.
Record this volume in cubic cm.

Measure the volume of a carton of milk or juice. You can measure the volume of the carton in cubic cm, but for the volume of liquids we use the term millilitre.
Millilitres (ml) and cubic cm (cm^3) are exactly the same.
A millilitre is one thousandth of a litre.

Look at liquid containers.
Are all of the contents measured in litres or ml rather than cubic cm?

One ml of pure water weighs one gramme (g).
Look for liquid containers.
What would be the weight of the water if each of the containers were filled with pure water?

Chapter 3 Density

Measuring the volume of your hand

Find a jug large enough for your hand to fit inside.
Half fill the jug with water.
Use sticky tape to mark this water level.
Put your fist inside the jug until the water covers your wrist.
Ask a friend to mark how high the water rises.
The water rises due to the volume of your fist.

Remove your fist from the jug.
Does the water return to its original level? If not, then some of the water stuck to your skin.
Add water to bring the water up to the original level.

Pour water from a measuring cylinder into the jug until the water level is at the second level.
How much water did you add?
What is the volume of your fist (see page 27)?
Does it matter if your hand is open or closed?

Is your right hand the same volume as your left hand?
Measure the volume of your friends' hands. How does the volume compare with the size that you measured on page 5?

Measuring your lung capacity

Put your hands on your ribs.
Breathe deeply in and out once.
What happens to your ribs?

Measure around a friend's chest.
Take the measurement when he is breathing out.
Measure again when he is breathing in.
How much does his chest expand?

Cut a strip of paper the height of a large plastic or glass bottle.
Use sticky tape to fasten your paper strip vertically to the outside of the bottle.
Fill the bottle with water.
Half fill the sink with water.
Ask an adult to help you turn the bottle upside down in the sink while still keeping the water in the bottle.
While the adult holds the bottle poke a length of plastic tubing into the neck of the bottle.

Take a deep breath. Pinch your nose and breathe out down the plastic tubing. Pinch the tube shut as soon as you have breathed out.
What volume of air is there in your bottle (see page 28)?

Measuring the volume of a stone

Put a jug full of water on the draining board of a sink.
Place a small wooden block under the jug to tilt it.
Notice that the water runs out of the spout.

Find a large stone that will fit inside the jug.
Tie thread around the stone.

Place an empty measuring cylinder or measuring jug beneath the spout of the tilted jug.

Slowly lower the stone into the water of the tilted jug until the stone is completely underwater.
Notice that water pours into your measuring cylinder.
The volume of water in the measuring cylinder equals the volume of the stone (see page 29).
How much water is there in your measuring cylinder?
What is the volume of your stone?

What is the weight of this volume of water (see page 27)?
Weigh the stone. Does the stone weigh the same as the water?

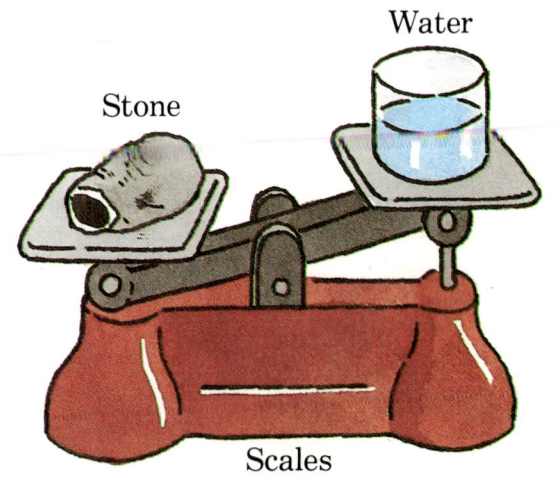

Repeat this exercise using different objects. What do you notice?

Measuring density

Find a measuring cylinder.
Put rice in the measuring cylinder.
Record the volume of rice.
Put this rice in a plastic bag.

Put the same volume of cornflakes in the measuring cylinder.
Put these cornflakes in another plastic bag.

Measure the same volume of sugar, dried peas, and sand.
Put these in their own plastic bags.

Measure the length of an unstretched strong rubber band.
Hang one of the bags with its contents on the end of your rubber band.
Measure the length of the stretched rubber band. Record this length.
Record the stretch of the rubber band for each bag.
Arrange your plastic bags according to their weights.

Notice that the weights of these substances you have measured are different, but their volumes are the same.
The heavier substances are denser.

The density of liquids

Half fill a glass with water.
Slowly pour some cooking oil into the water in the glass.
What happens?
Let the liquids stand.
Which is the heavier liquid?
This liquid is the denser liquid (see page 31).

Float an empty plastic tub on water.
Is the plastic tub less dense than water?
Add a small amount of sand to the plastic tub.
Measure the water level on the side of the tub.
What happens when you add a little more sand to the tub?
Is the tub of sand less dense than water?
What happens when the tub of sand is more dense than the water?

Look for trucks and tankers carrying liquids.
Why are cement tankers smaller than milk tankers?